Biel Goes Shopping

+

Who Blocked My Nose?

Published by BnMs Empire LTD
bnmsempire@gmail.com
www.comestudywithme.com

© BnMs Empire LTD 2017

All rights reserved. Without limiting the rights under copyright reserved above, no

part of this publication may be reproduced, stored in or introduced into a retrieval system, or transmitted in any form or by any form or by any means (electronic, mechanical, photocopying, recording or otherwise), without the prior written permission of both the copyright owner and the above publisher of this book.

A catalogue record of this book is available from the British Library.

ISBN: 978-1-9998912-0-6

For Malachi and Biel

This book belongs to ……………………………………..

From……………………………………………………………..

Biel Goes Shopping

Biel went shopping with his mummy and big brother today.

What did he see?

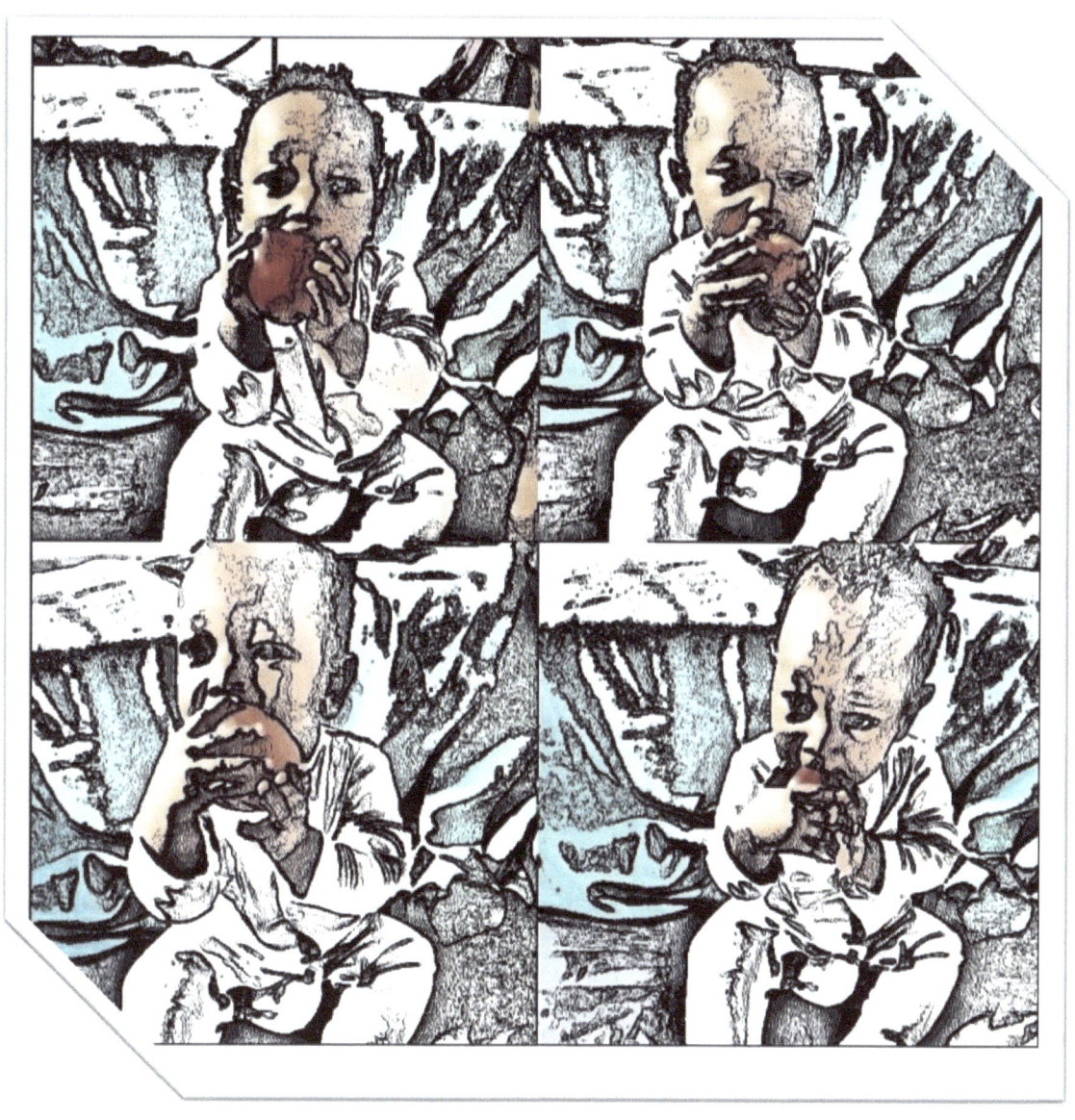

Biel saw an apple that went straight in his tummy.

Biel saw some small things that looked like stones.

Mummy called it rice.

He sure hope it tasted nice.

Then Biel saw his favourite thing......

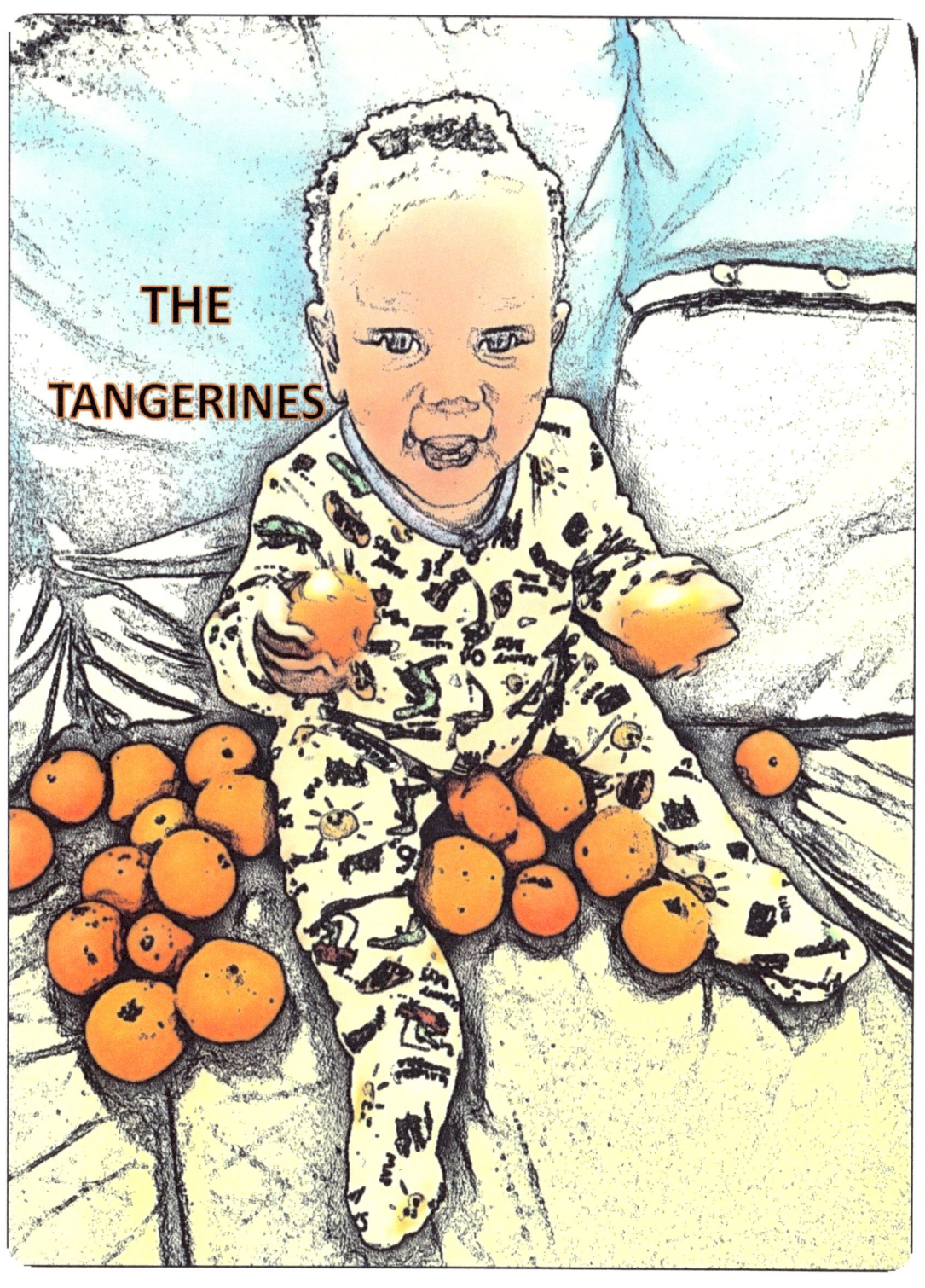

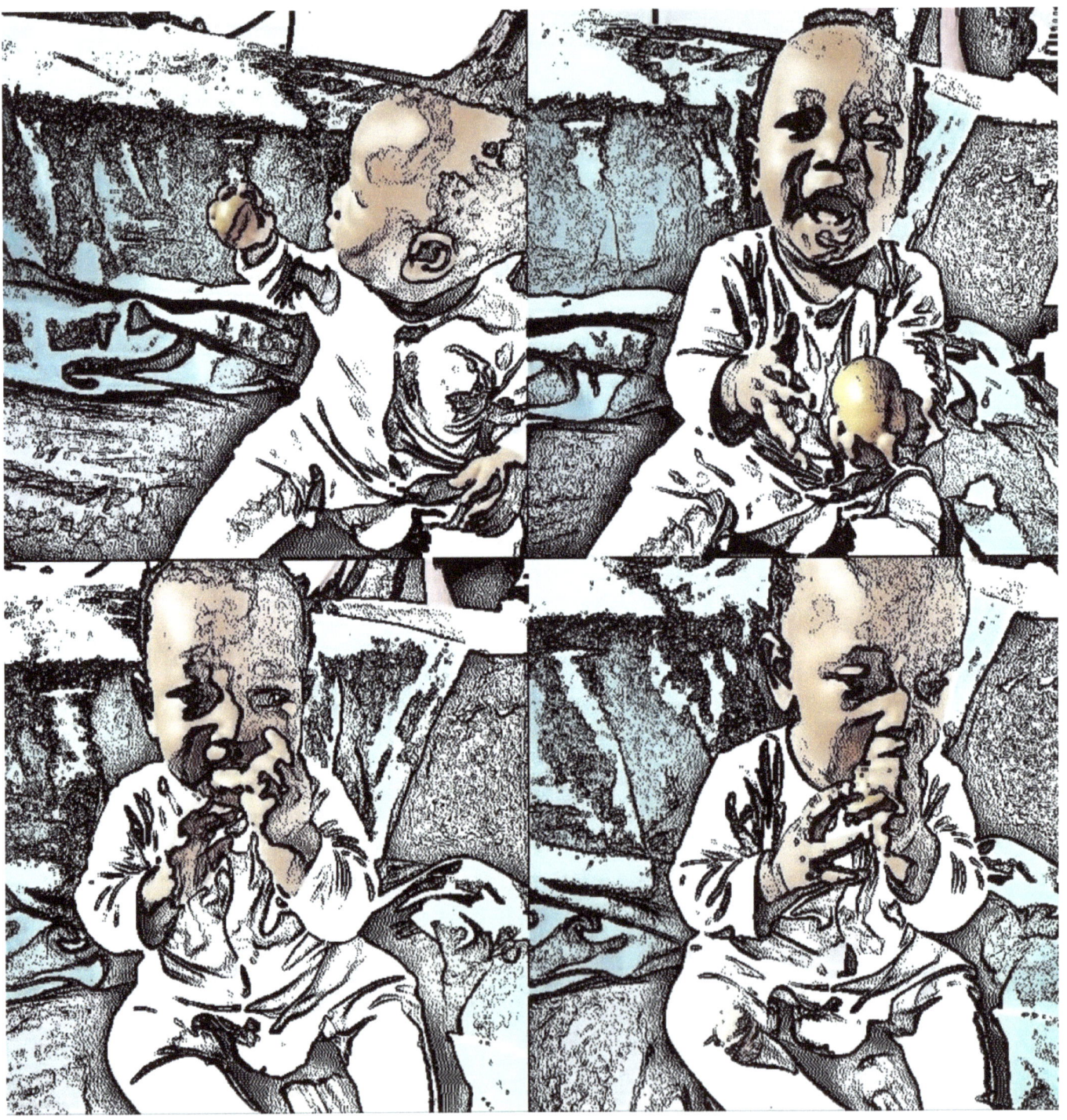

Who Blocked My Nose?

Who blocked my nose?

Help! Help!

My nose is all stuffy.

Did something crawl in there to make it go puffy?

Who blocked my nose?

Was it my brother that blocked up my nose? Was it the time he blew bubbles and that's why it closed?

Was it my daddy that blocked up my nose?

When he tickled my belly I giggled and giggled.

I pulled on his beard while I wiggled and wiggled.

Did hair fall from his beard into my nose?

It probably did I suppose.

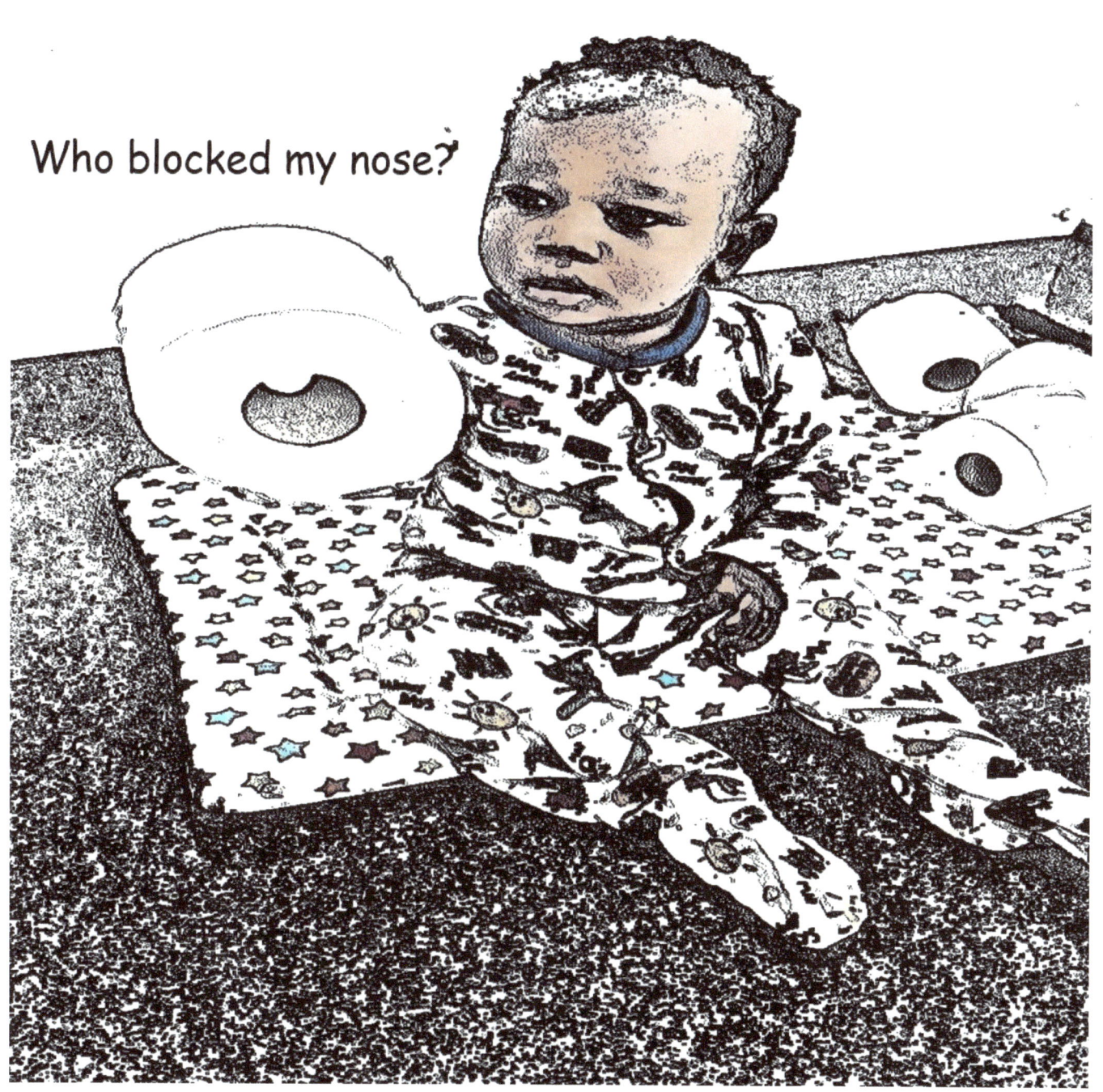

Was it my mummy who blocked up my nose?

The smoke from our meal just rose and rose.

Did the scent reach to me where I was looking?

Now I'm all blocked up because of the cooking.

Who blocked my nose?

My mummy dabbed oil on my vest this evening.

Wow what a difference that made to my breathing.

That oil really did save the day.
To keep my blocked nose at bay.

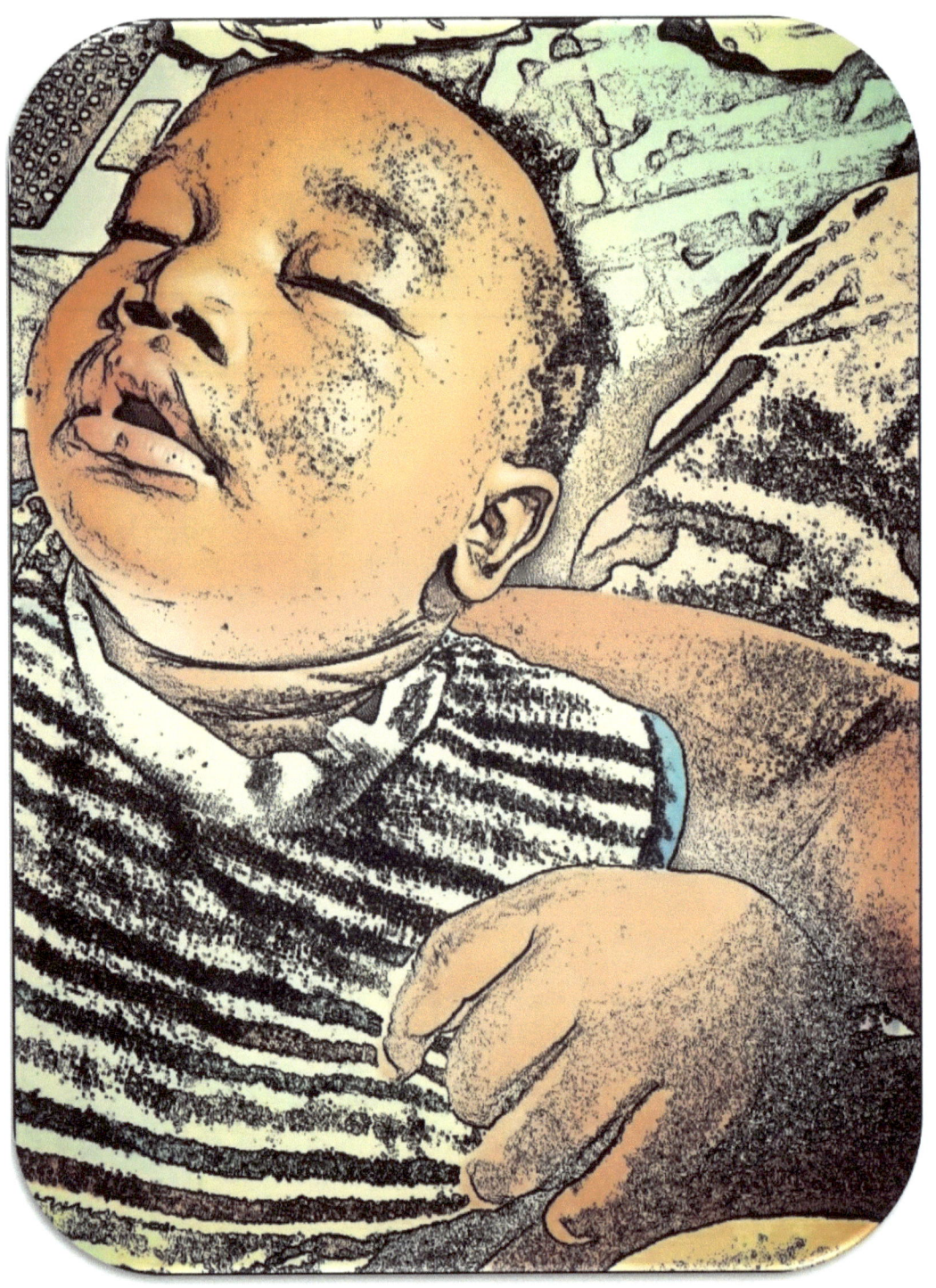

As I laid my head to get some sleep, I opened my eyes to take one more peep.

At my family I love from my head to my toes.

I knew deep down they would have never blocked my nose.

www.ingramcontent.com/pod-product-compliance
Lightning Source LLC
Chambersburg PA
CBHW041232040426

42444CB00002B/139